Creative Challenges for C...

SCAVENGER ART

Written by Lexi Rees

Illustrated by Molly O'Donoghue

Published in Great Britain
By Outset Publishing Ltd

First edition published November 2020

Written by Lexi Rees
Illustrated by Molly O'Donoghue

ISBN:978-1-913799-04-5

www.lexirees.co.uk

HOW to USE THIS JOURNAL

Scavenger hunts are fun

Drawing is fun

Both encourage us to look at the world around us more closely. They're also a way for us to practise mindfulness, by being in the present moment, noticing things we might otherwise rush past, focusing on them as we draw, and taking the time to appreciate them.

Each scavenger hunt has a grid with nine little boxes. Your challenge is to fill each box with a different sketch that fits the theme.

Don't worry about how perfect your drawing is - it's a scavenger hunt, not an art competition!

How many can you complete?
Have fun!

Lexi and Molly

1

MY HOUSE

MY BEDROOM

You could draw the furniture, but to make
this scavenger hunt harder, look for
smaller things.

Stand in the middle of your room and turn around slowly.
What do you see?

A lamp, the curtains, a rug, a bookshelf...
How small can you go? Now look again...
A light switch, a plug socket, a light bulb, a clothes hook.

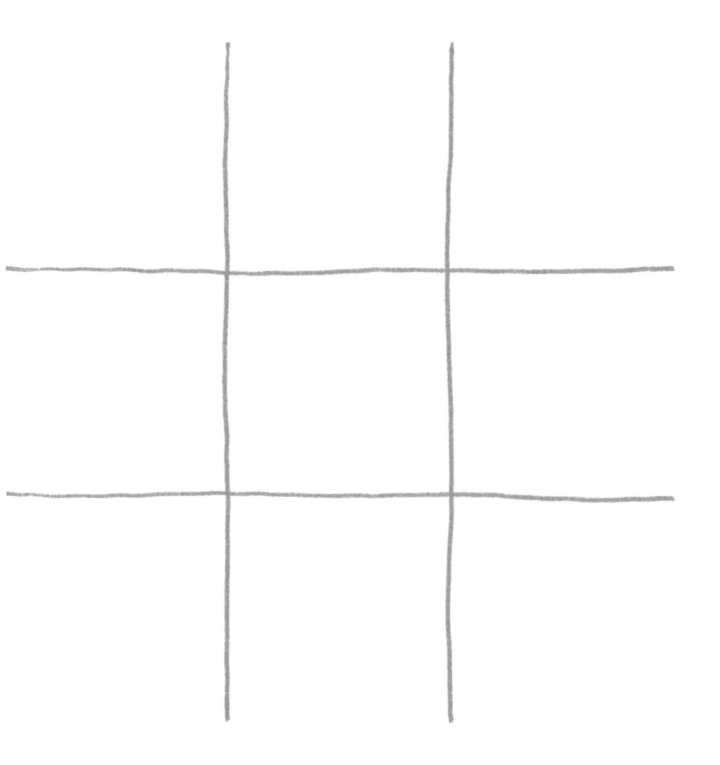

VIEWS FROM WINDOWS

For this scavenger hunt, start by drawing the view from every room in your house.

Notice how the perspective looks slightly different from each window. If you have space left on the grid, what about the views from a friend's house? Or from your classroom.

(But don't doodle during lessons).

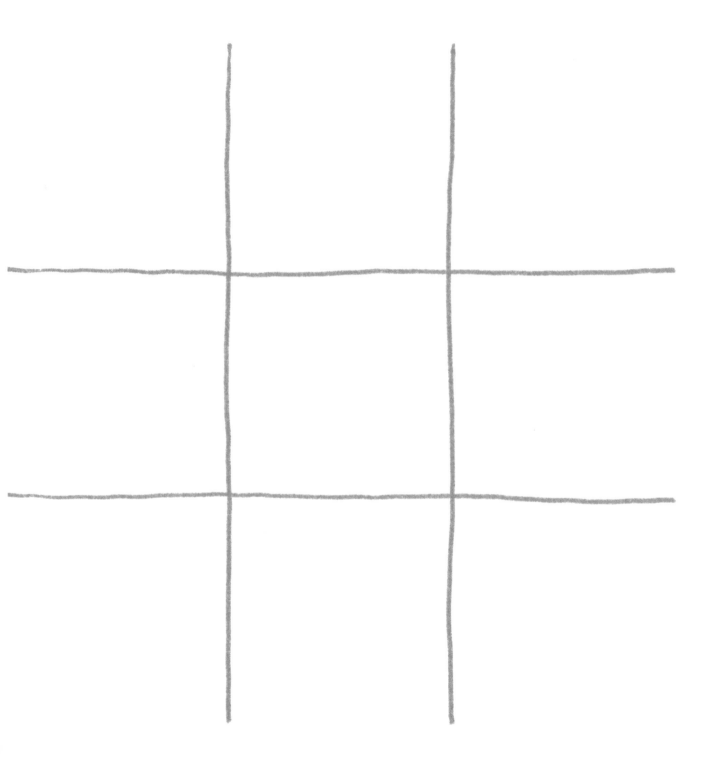

MUGS and JUGS

How many different shapes
and styles can you find?

Bonus points for drawing any chipped crockery —
things don't need to be in perfect condition to be
worthy of drawing.

Please don't break anything, we don't want to get into trouble :)
Molly and Lexi

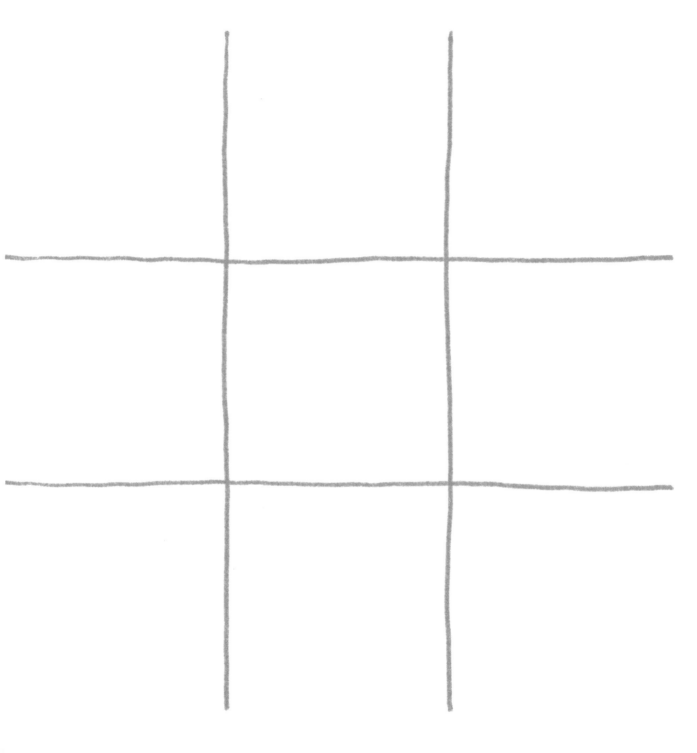

GLASSES

Tall glasses, short glasses, fancy crystal glasses, wine glasses, cocktail glasses.

We were already worried about the crockery, but now we're really worried about the glasses! Please don't break anything :)
Molly and Lexi

BOOKS

Bulging bookshelves?

Bedside tables piled high?

Spilling out of school bags?

Perhaps in the bathroom!

To complete this scavenger hunt, either draw all the different places where books are kept in your house or copy your favourite book covers. It's up to you.

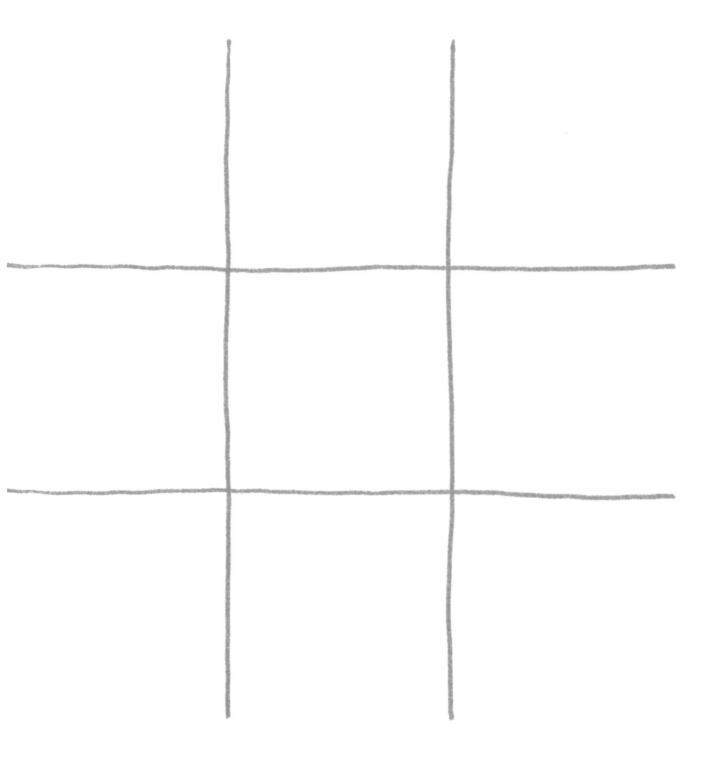

KNICK KNACKS

Curate a collection of curious objects to complete this challenge.

Have you ever looked at the ornaments and knick-knacks your family have collected over the years?

Souvenirs from holidays?

Weird shaped objects you made when you were little?

Fancy photo frames?

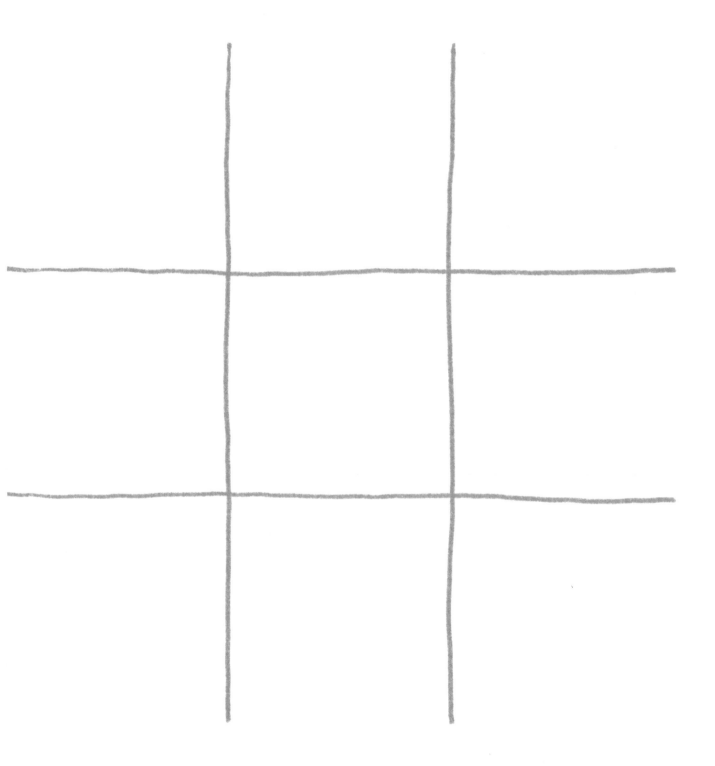

PICTURES and PAINTINGS

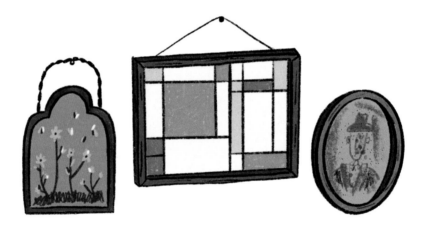

Be inspired by the most famous artists in the world! Can you create your own versions of some of their paintings?

Van Gogh's sunflowers, Degas' ballet dancers, Constable's landscapes, Monet's waterlilies, Frida Kahlo's brightly-coloured self-portraits, Dali's surreal melting clocks.

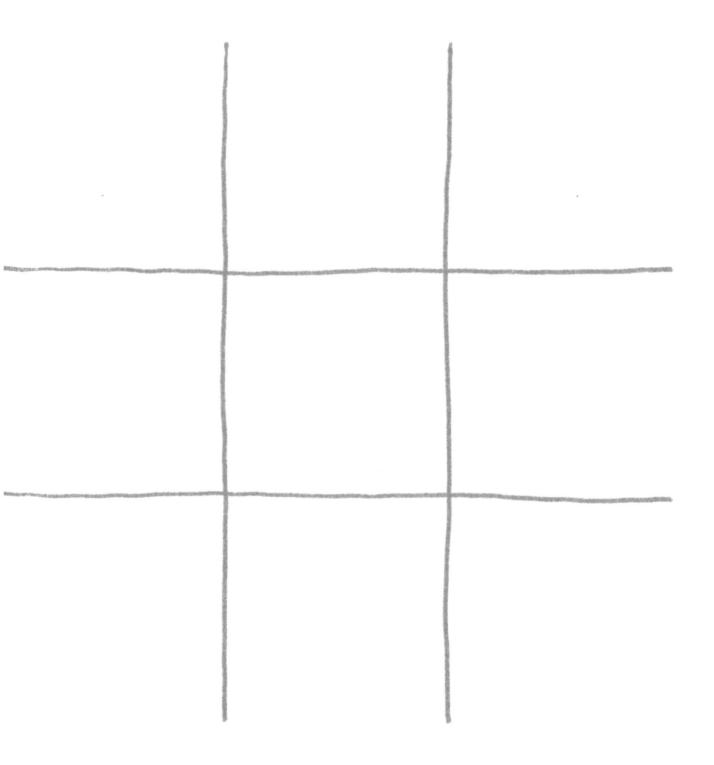

POTTED PLANTS

If your family has green fingers, you might be able to complete this challenge in your own house or garden.

All is not lost if you struggle to keep a cactus alive.

As you walk along the street, keep an eye out for window boxes, or a plant pot by the front door?

Or next time you're in a café or restaurant see if they use any plants as decoration. Look closely - are they real or plastic? Sometimes it can be hard to tell!

MY STUFF

TOYS

There are lots of options here, but you can make the challenge harder by picking a theme:

My favourite toys
Toys I would invent if I was a designer
Toys for babies
Wooden toys
Toys I don't play with anymore

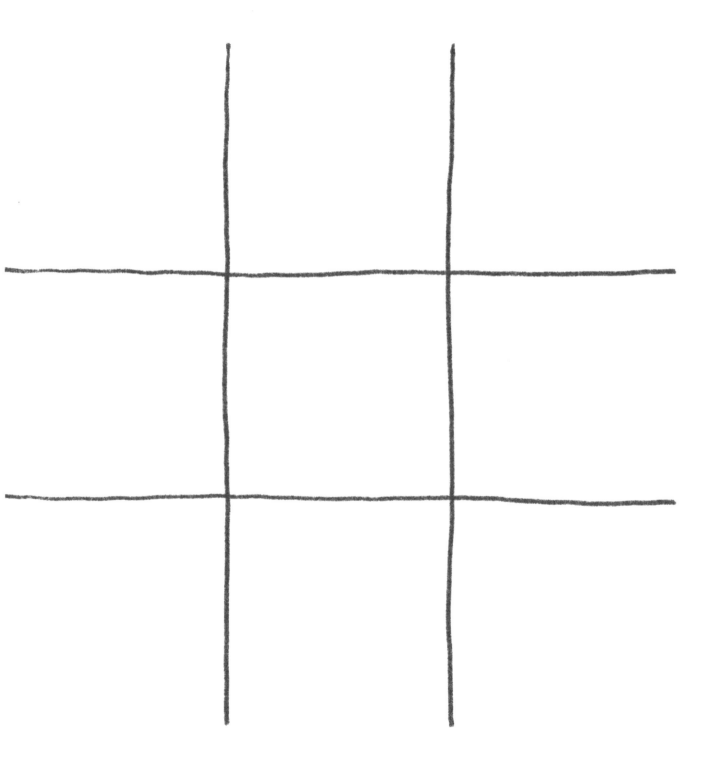

CLOTHES

You could draw them lying flat, folded on a shelf or in a drawer, or on a hanger?

If it's difficult to choose, why not find a theme?
Your favourite clothes
Summer clothes
Winter clothes
Clothes with patterns

Molly's Tip
Try to use shading to show the wrinkles and creases in the clothes.

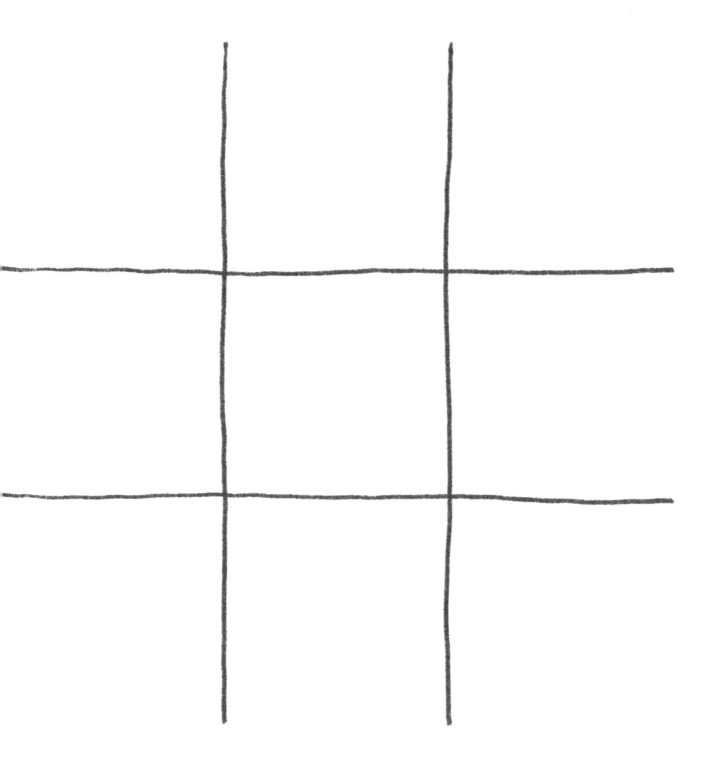

SOCKS

Spotty or stripey

Frilly or fancy

Old and smelly

(maybe leave those ones in the laundry basket)

Molly's Tip.
Add wiggly lines for extra smelly socks or flowers for those that have just come out of the wash!

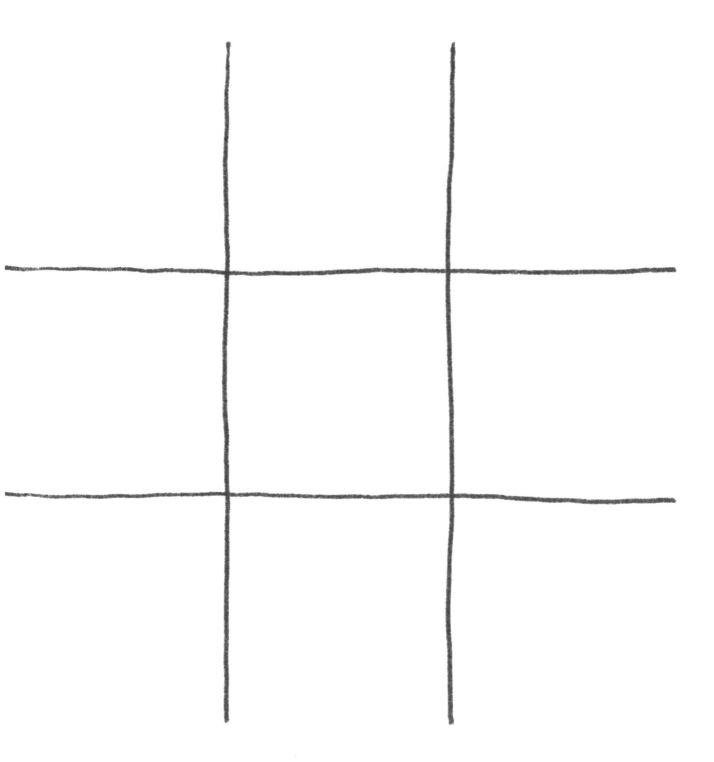

SHOES

There are so many different types
to choose from.

football boots,
ballet shoes, school shoes,
welly boots, trainers, flip flops,
high heels, tall boots, baby shoes.

To make this scavenger hunt harder, find different sizes
and styles for every box.

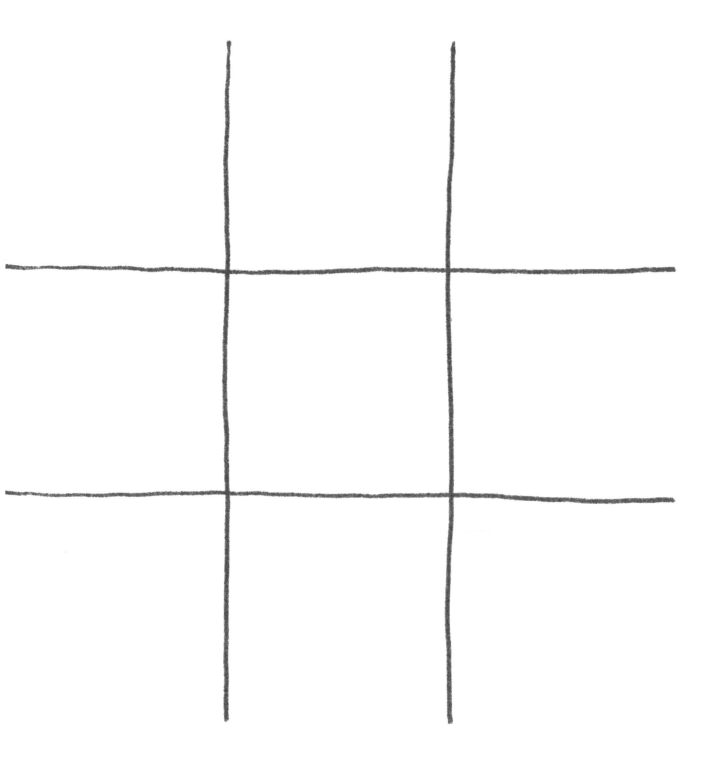

BAGS

For this challenge, you could start with your school bag.

What about a carrier bag overflowing with shopping?

Or your mum's favourite handbag?

The big suitcase with wheels you bring on holiday?

A muddy bag with football kit in it?

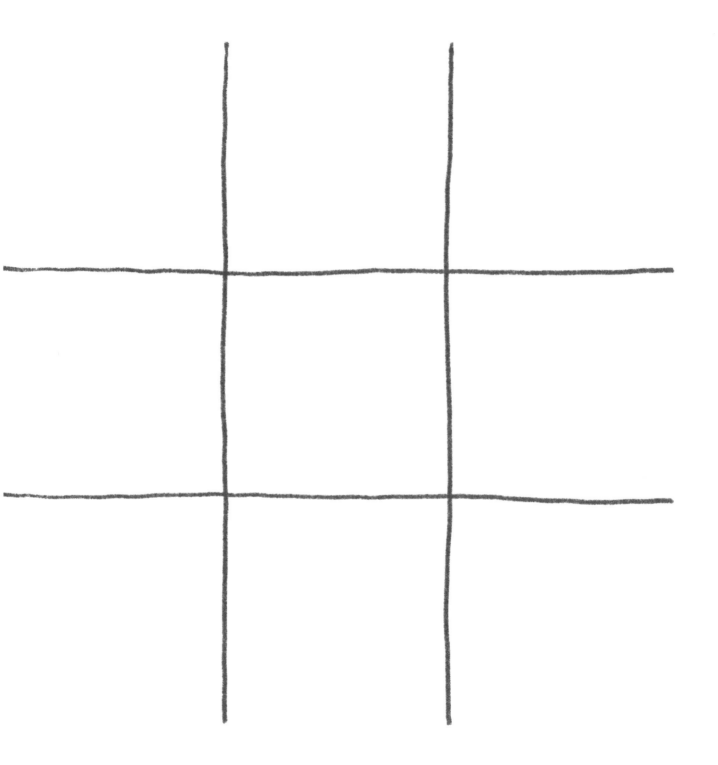

BADGES and BUTTONS

Buttons come in all shapes and sizes.
Can you find some unusual ones?

Have you ever looked closely at the buttons on a
pair of jeans? They often have writing on them –
what does it say?

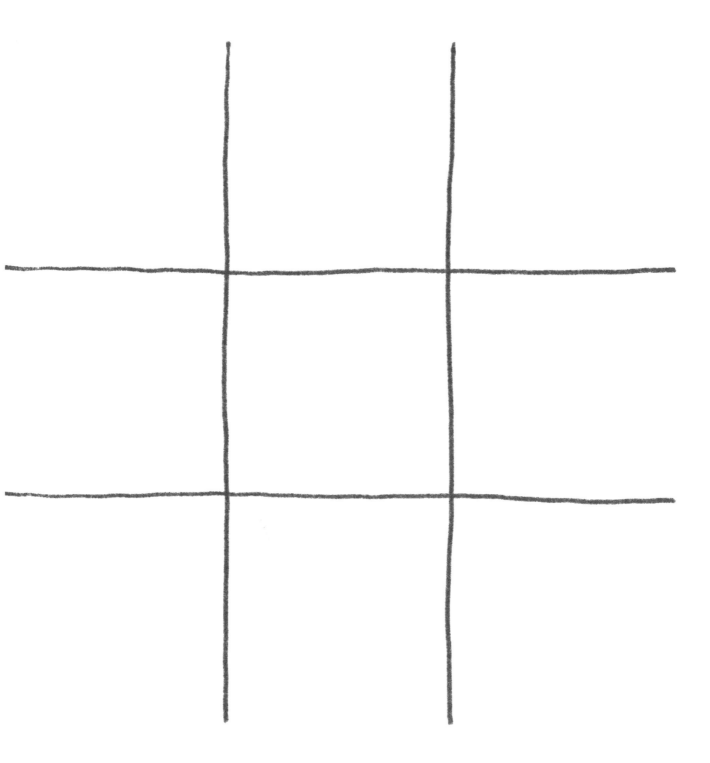

GEMS and JEWELS

Most of us don't own a diamond tiara
(maybe you do), but what sparkly things
can you find?

Molly's tip.
Hold the jewel up to the light and see it sparkle, use small diamond
shapes in your drawings to show how it glistens.

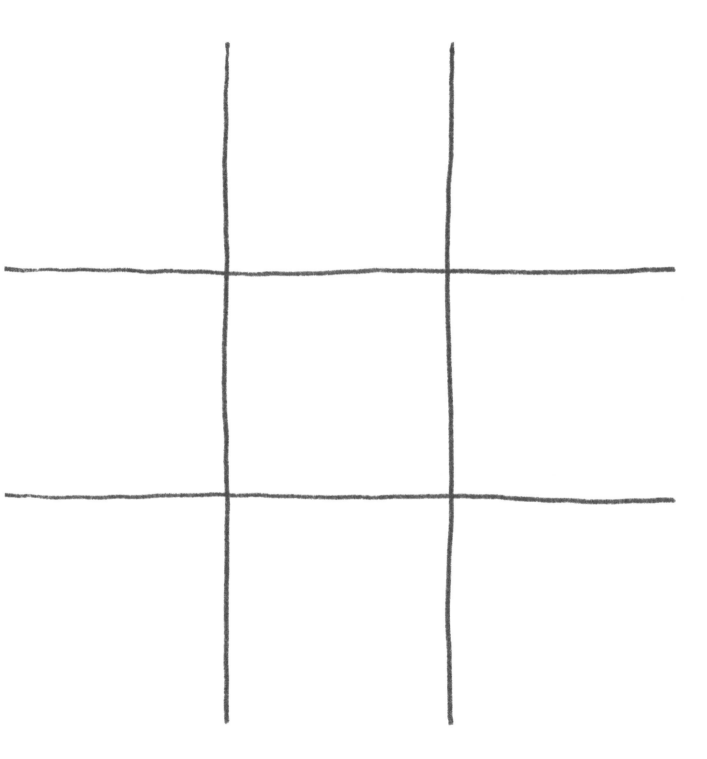

OUTSIDE

FRONT DOORS

Can you find some interesting doors?

Look for fancy door knockers, glass panes, wood panels, letterboxes. Or stand back and look for doors with ornate porches or steps leading up to them.

Don't forget to look at shops, offices, churches, and other buildings, as well as houses.

WINDOW FRAMES

We are usually so busy looking through the window, we forget to look at the window itself.

Keep your eyes open for unique details like the handles and latches. If you live near a church, you might even be able to find some stained-glass windows with patterned panes.

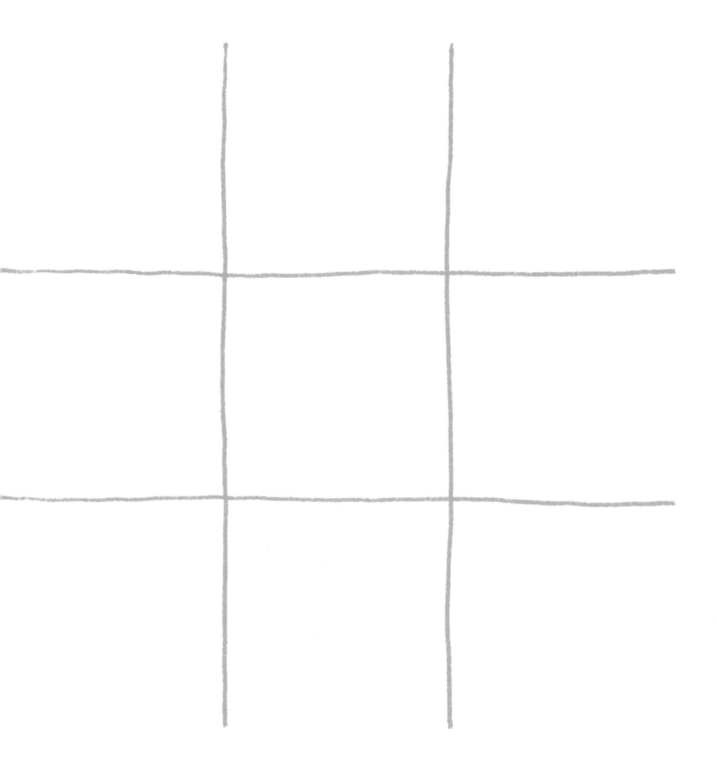

ROOFTOPS

You'll have to go upstairs to complete this scavenger hunt. Binoculars might help too!

Most of us have slates or tiles, but maybe you live somewhere where there are thatched roofs.

Can you spot the ridge tiles? Are there any finials?

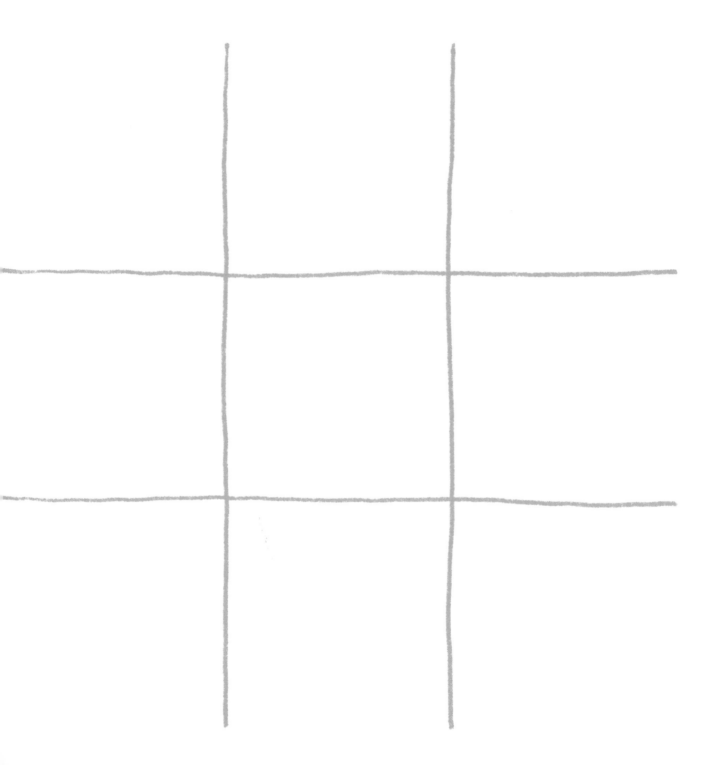

SKYLINES

To get bonus points in this scavenger hunt, look out for striking features like church spires and steeples, tall trees, and skyscrapers.

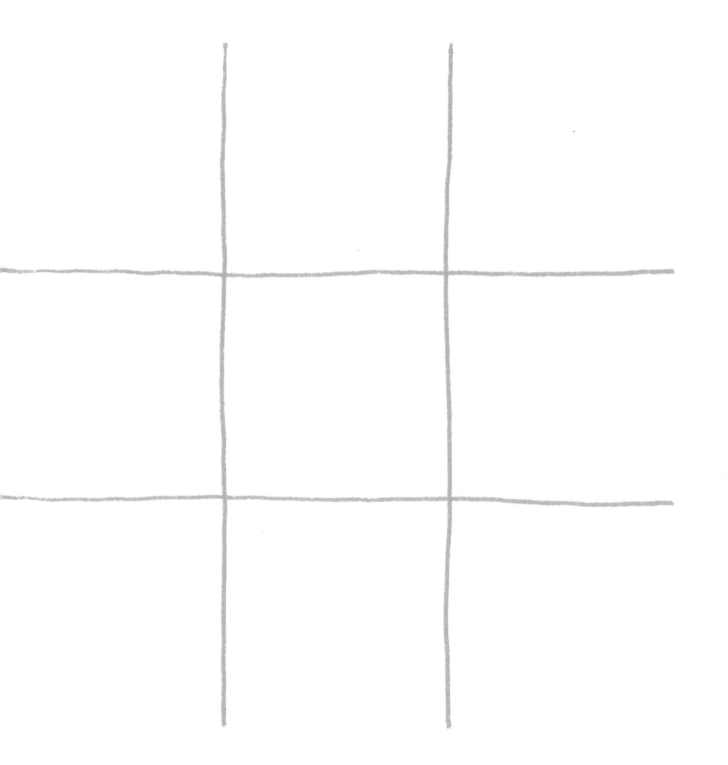

SHOP FRONTS

Next time you're shopping,
look at all the different shop fronts.

What about the window displays?

Are there stickers in the window saying 'Sale'
or special holiday decorations?

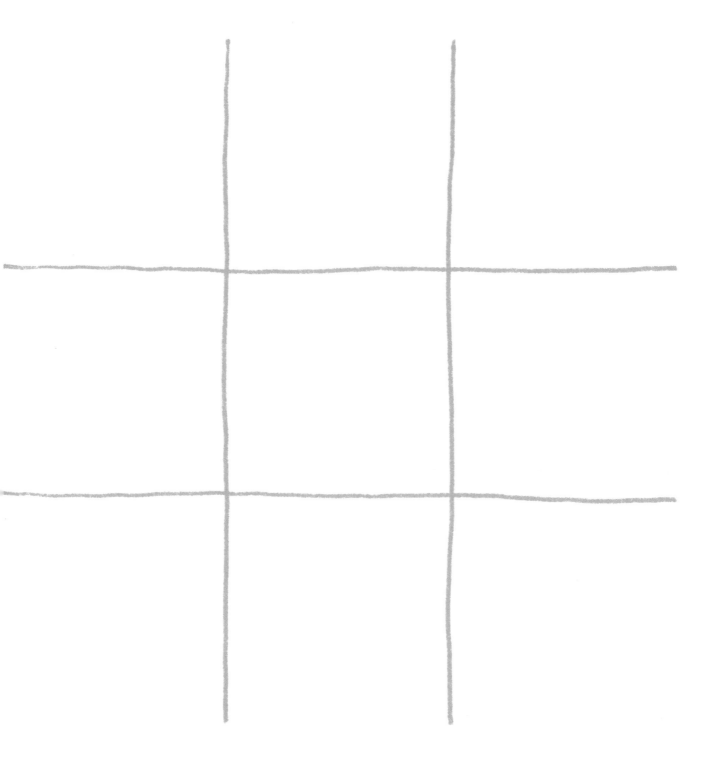

FENCES and GATES

From curly wrought iron to rustic oak,
how many different styles can you find?

Some are quite plain and others ornate,

where can you find the most colourful gate?

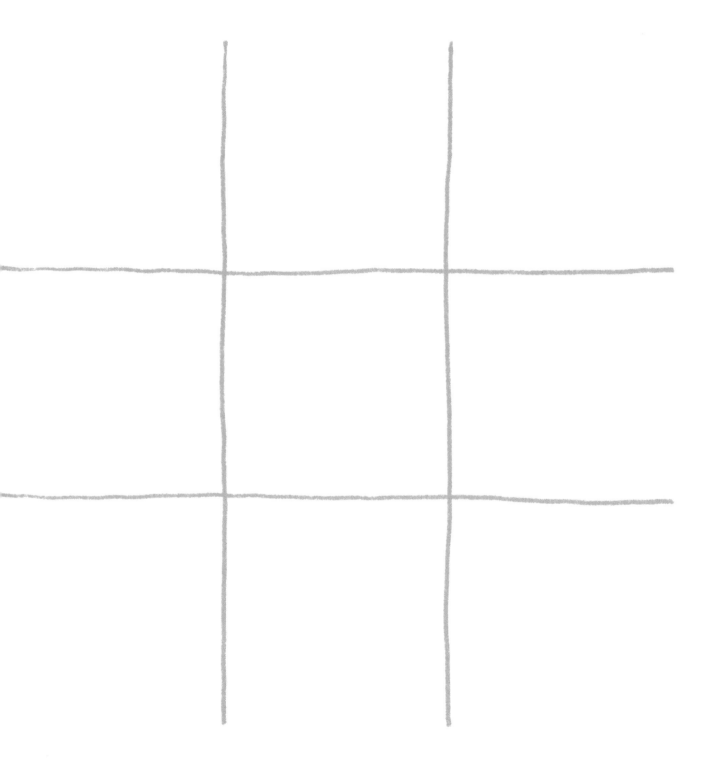

VEHICLES

Cars, buses, trucks, vans, tractors...

If it has an engine, it's in this scavenger hunt!

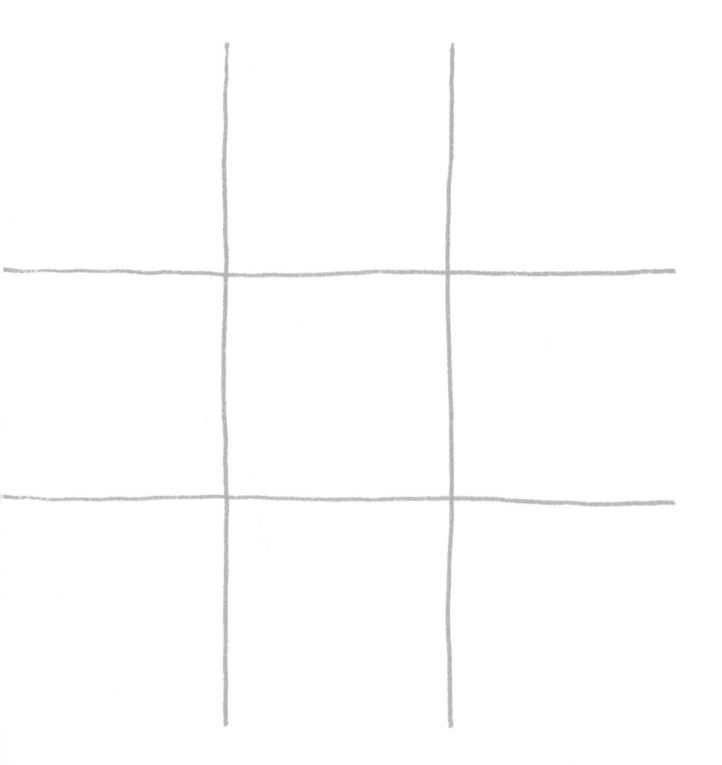

PEOPLE

FAMILY

Can you find any old photos of your ancestors?

See if you can spot any similarities to yourself or your siblings.

That's genetics!

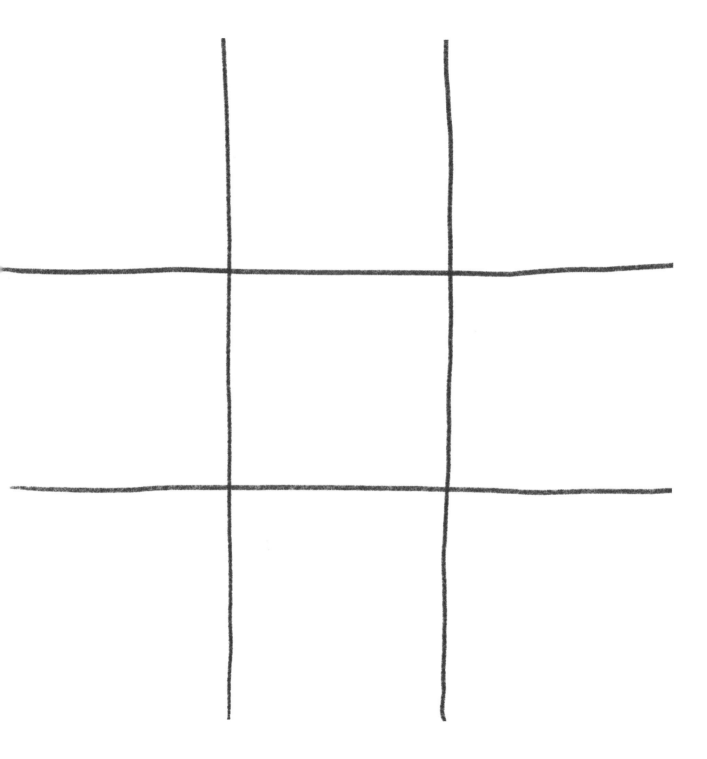

FRIENDS

Try to bring out the personality of each of your friends in their portraits.

Maybe include something to represent a hobby or their favourite thing, like a football or an ice-cream.

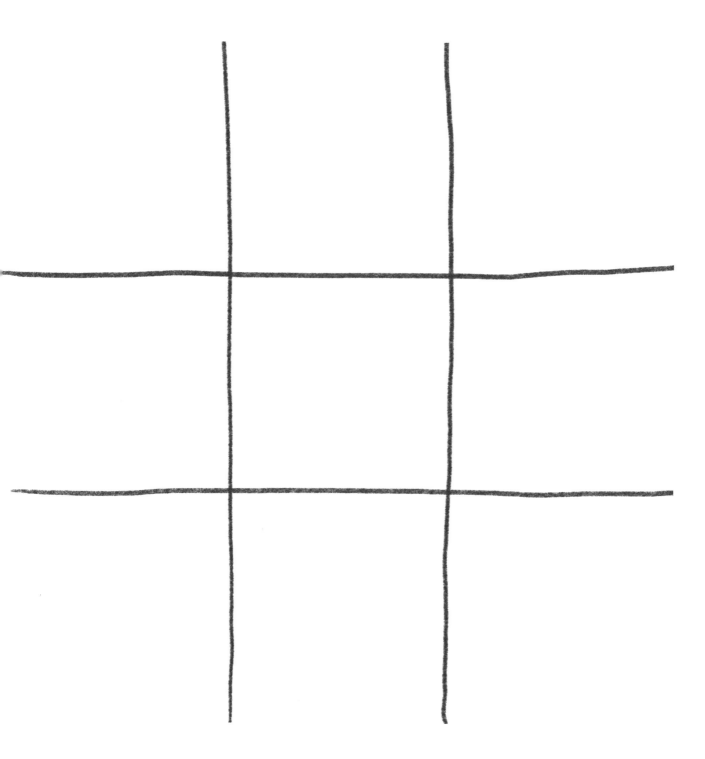

FUNNY FACES

If you have a mirror,
you can do silly self-portraits.

Or have fun with your friends and family.

Who pulls the funniest faces?

Can you capture their crazy expressions?

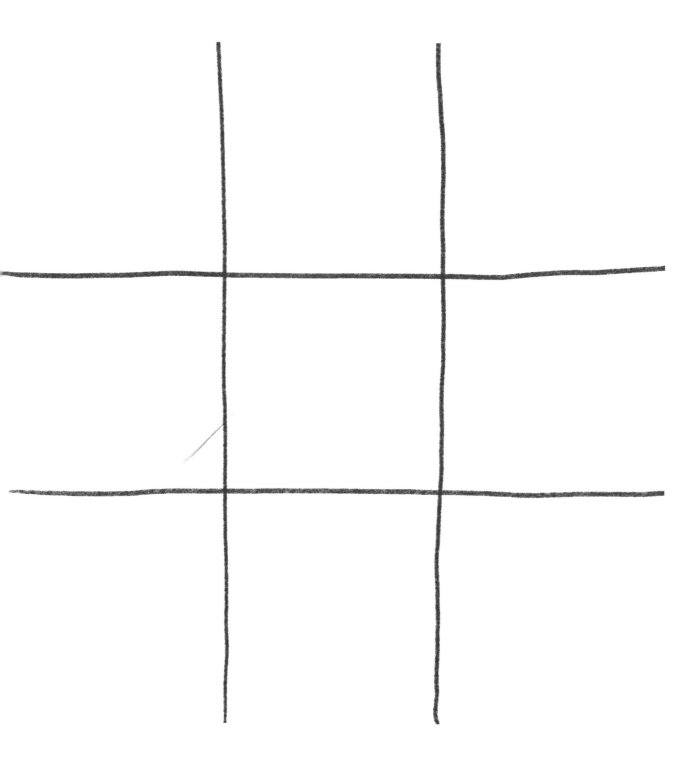

PEOPLE in HATS

Winter hats

Sun hats

Safety hats

Party hats

A Santa hat

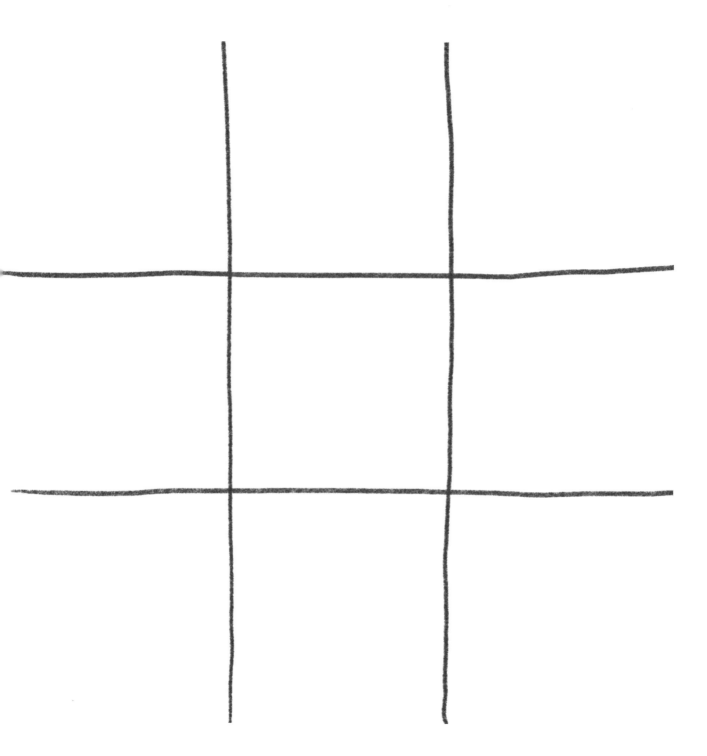

PEOPLE at WORK

Who can you see at work?

a teacher, a shop assistant, a receptionist, a hairdresser,
a fireman, a delivery person, a nurse?

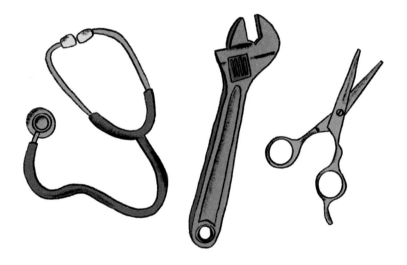

Bonus Challenge: include something that represents their job in the picture.

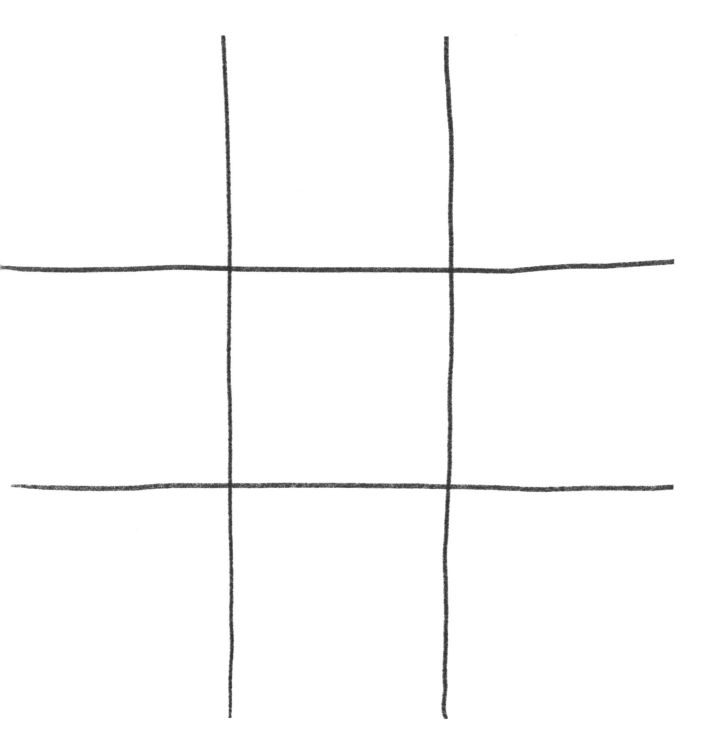

PLAYING SPORTS

How many different sports can you see people doing?

running, cycling, swimming, diving, football, tennis, hula hooping, dancing, fencing, gymnastics, horse riding, basketball, rugby, hockey.

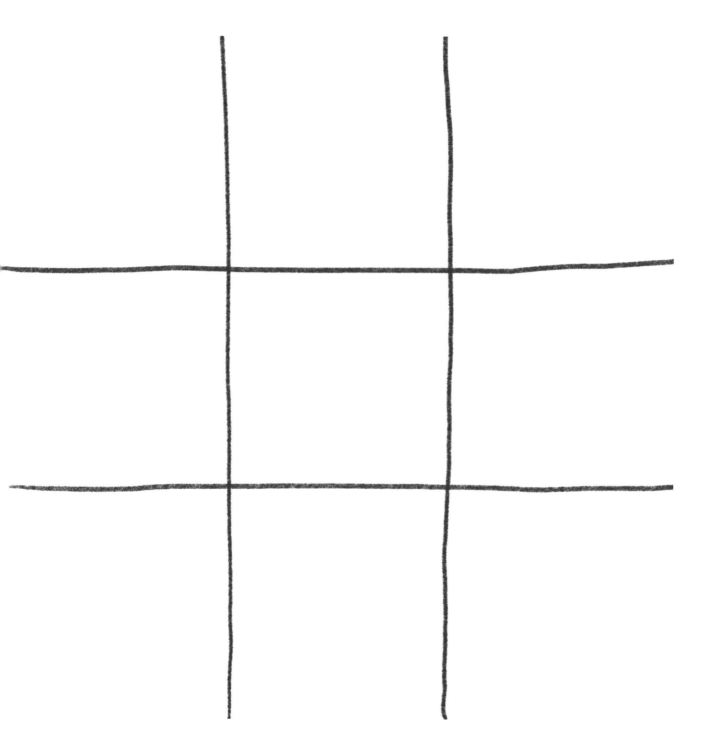

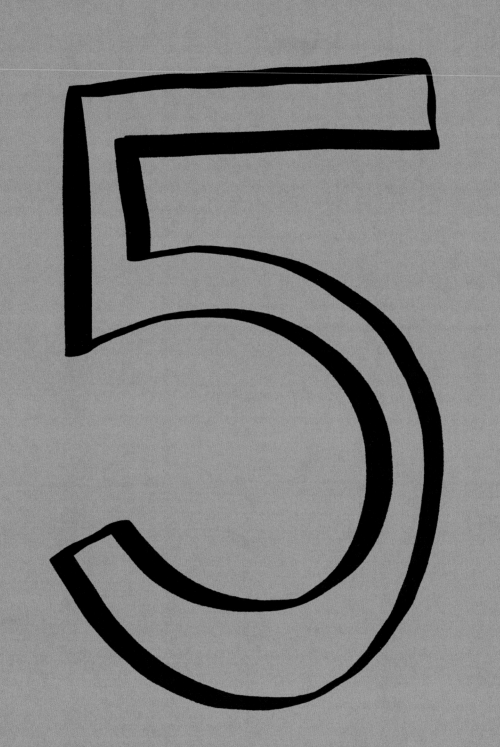

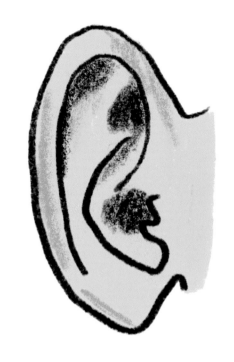

FACES and BODIES

EYES

When you look at a person, the first thing you might notice is the colour of their eyes.

Now look at the shape of their eyebrows –
are they bushy or thin? Arched or straight?
Or maybe so overgrown it's become a monobrow?
(Aren't they fashionable at the moment?)

Do they have luscious, long eyelashes or short,
stubby ones?

What about the eyelids? Are they droopy or wide?

EARS

For this scavenger hunt, you need to draw lots of different ears from babies to old people. Write the person's age under the sketch and compare them afterwards.

Have you ever been told that your ears never stop growing? That's not quite true!

Bones stop growing, but ears are made from cartilage which continues to grow throughout our lives.

But the main reason your ears get bigger is that as we get older, gravity takes its toll and earlobes get droopy and saggy!

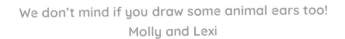

We don't mind if you draw some animal ears too!
Molly and Lexi

NOSES

Just like ears, there is cartilage in noses so they seem to grow over time.

You might need a coloured pencil as some people's noses go red in the cold... or even turn blue!

Can you find someone with a cute button nose?

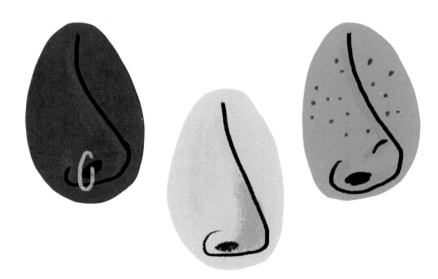

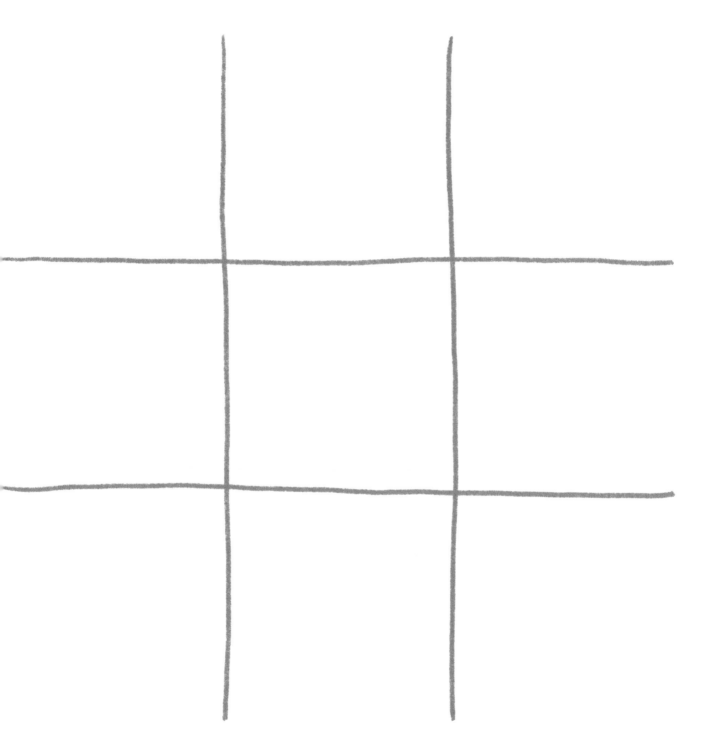

HAIRSTYLES

How many different hairstyles
can you capture?

Long or short,

Straight or curly,

Slicked down or spiked up,

Pink, green, black, brown, or grey.

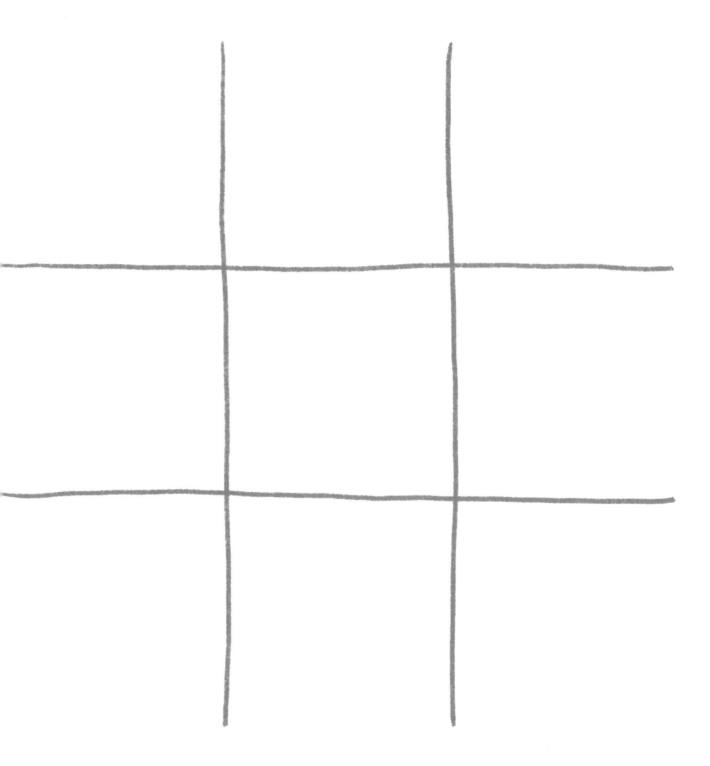

HANDS

Can you draw your hand in
nine different poses?

holding a pencil

clenched into a fist

pointing a finger

thumbs up or thumbs down

Give us a wave!

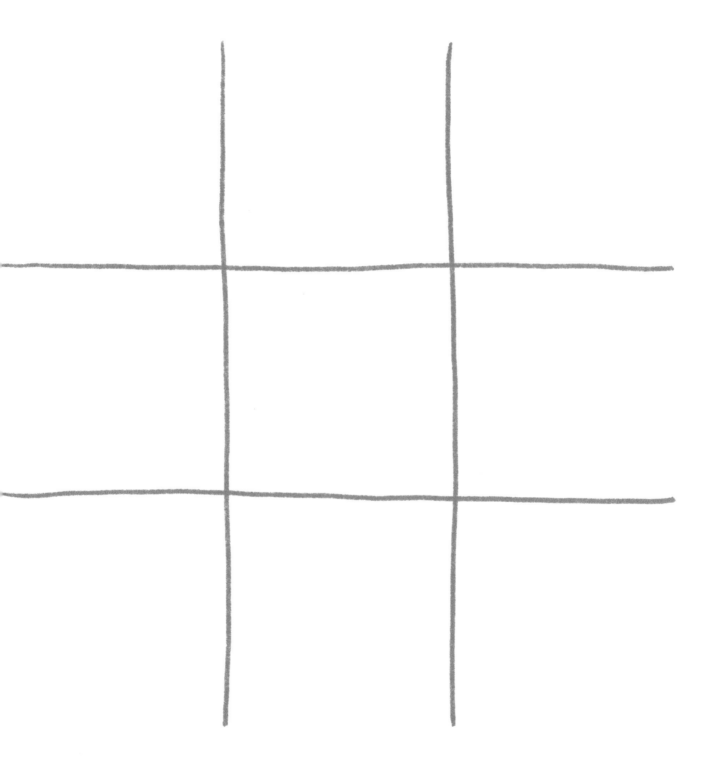

FEET

Feet are often funnily shaped,
with wonky toes and curves and bumps.

Can you draw your foot whilst standing on one leg?

Don't fall over!

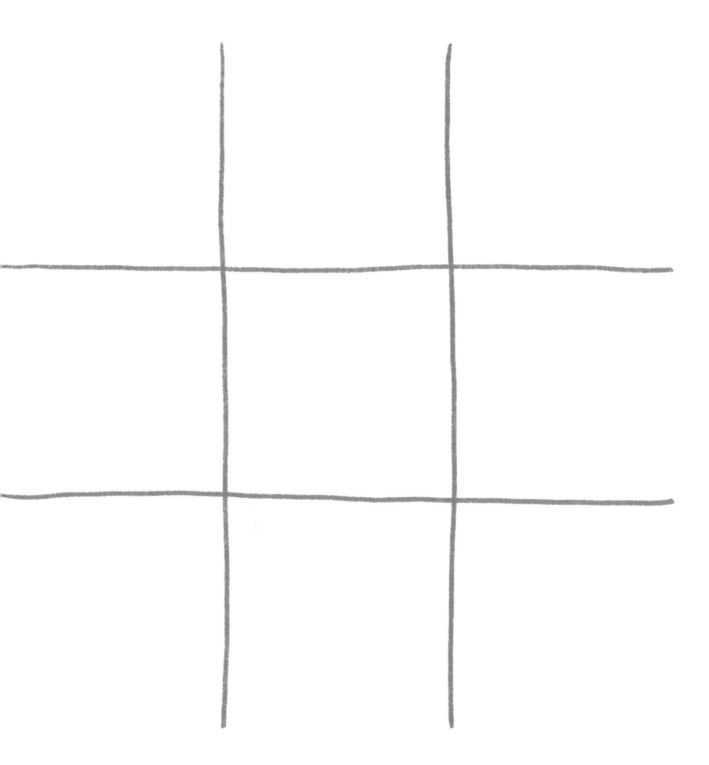

NATURE

LEAVES

Every tree has a unique shape of leaf.

How many different shapes can you find?
Draw them outside, or take them home to draw later.

Can you identify them? Label each of your drawings with
the type of tree the leaf comes from.

FLOWERS

They might be in a vase, at the park,
or in a garden.

Even if they are technically weeds, like thistles,
they can still have beautiful flowers that bloom.

Please don't pick wild flowers, leave them for others to enjoy too!

CLOUDS

Clouds make weird and wonderful patterns.
What do you see in them?

Can you draw those wacky shapes?

TREES

How many different shapes and types of trees can you find? Here are some ideas:

Tall thin poplars

Droopy willows

Colourful autumn maples

Bristly firs

Bulging baobabs

Or you could follow a tree through the seasons.

Bonus points if you can find a dead tree stump!

BARK
TEXTURES

From gnarled and knobbly to smooth and flaky, bark has lots of really interesting textures to draw.

SEEDS and PIPS

When you're out for a walk, look on the ground for horse chestnuts (conkers) and acorns, as long as the squirrels haven't buried them all. Can you see any flying seeds like sycamore wings and dandelion fluff?

Or you could do this scavenger hunt inside. Next time you eat an apple, draw the core. Have you ever counted the number of pips in a slice of watermelon?

Raid your kitchen cupboards. Sunflower seeds? Sesame seeds? Cumin seeds? Peppercorns? It's enough for the weirdest feast.

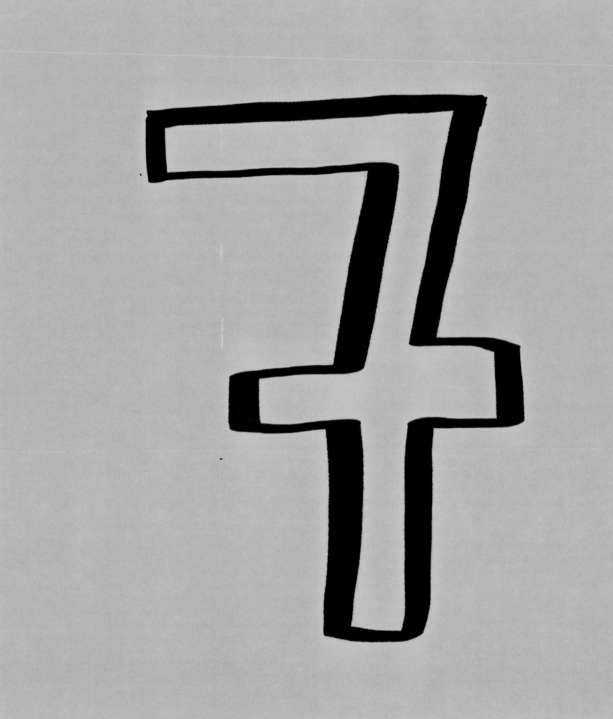

EATING

FRUIT

Different fruits are harvested each season.

Think of the locally grown fruits
in your area.

Compare them to exotic fruits from
another country.

**Can you make this page an exuberance
of colours and shapes?**

PASTA SHAPES

Long or short, fat or thin, straight or curly.

Each different pasta shape has a special name.
Can you label your drawings?

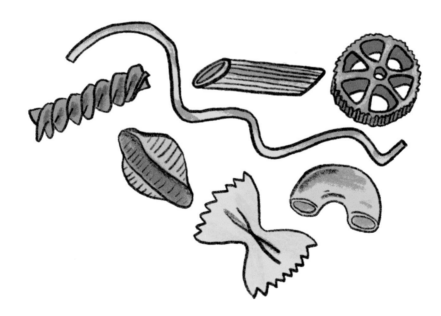

NUTS

In the shell or out of the shell, like snowflakes, you'll never find two the same.

If anyone in your household is allergic to nuts, replace this challenge with a FREE CHOICE.

Write your alternative topic here.

· · · · · · · · · · · · · · · · · · · ·

PACKETS and PACKAGING

Make a note under each if it's recyclable or not.

BREAKFAST CEREALS

Flat, round, bumpy, flaky.
This scavenger hunt is all about
shapes and textures.

We admit it, we like to eat breakfast cereals at any time of day!
Lexi and Molly

SWEETS and CANDIES

Have you ever noticed how you can recognise a sweet by the wrapper?

So many treats, so bad for our teeth.

How many different sweets and wrappers can you find?

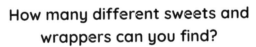

Warning: don't eat them all at once. And brush your teeth!

BIRDS, INSECTS, and ANIMALS

DOGS

How many different breeds of
dogs can you find?

Label each dog with its name and the correct breed.

CATS

Have you read any of the poems in
Old Possum's Book of Practical Cats by
T.S. Eliot? They're great fun.

P.S. Watch out for cute kittens –
don't fall under their spell!

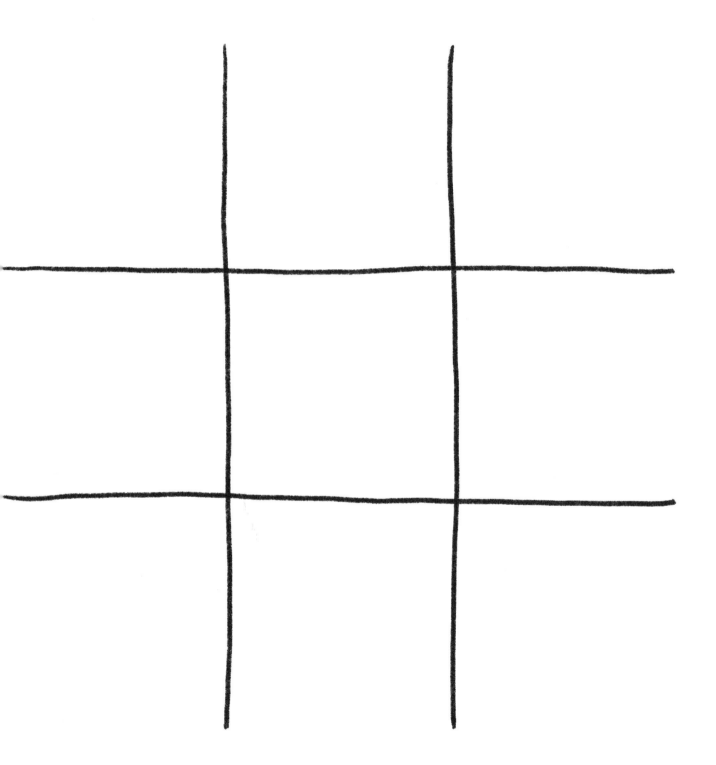

BIRDS

To complete this challenge, see how many different types of bird you can find.

You'll need to draw quickly as they won't stay still for long.

Do you have a bird feeder?

Even if you don't have a garden or balcony, you can get ones that attach to windows with suction cups.

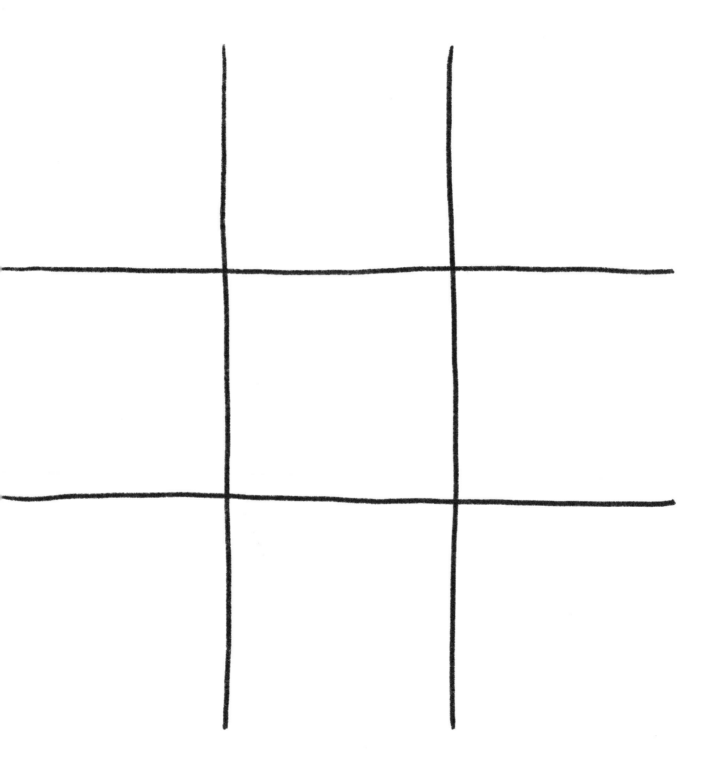

INSECTS

Beautiful or ugly? Friendly or annoying?

Flies, bees, wasps, gnats, dragonflies, butterflies.
They all play a vital role in the ecosystem.

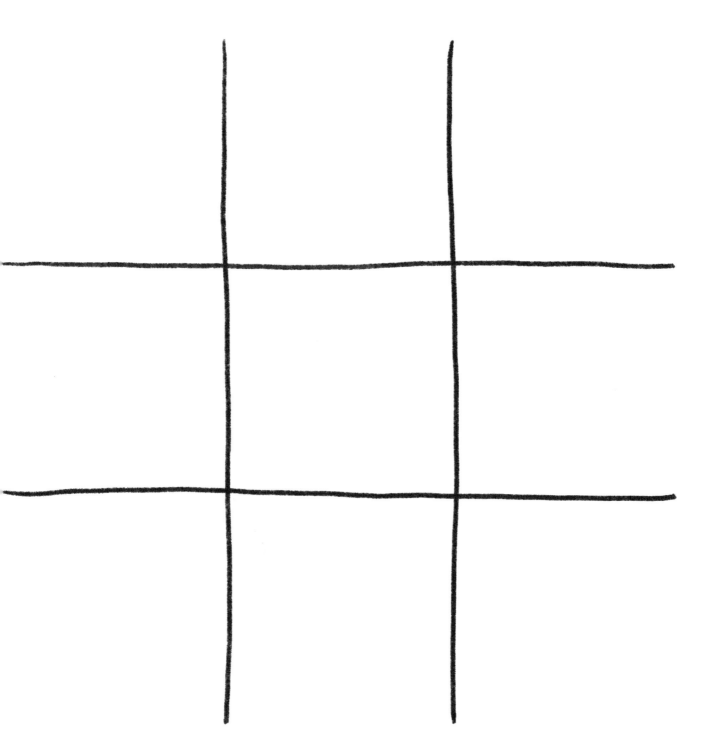

CREEPY CRAWLIES

Worms and spiders,
Bugs and beetles,
Slugs and snails.

Can you find one that is multi-coloured?

OTHER ANIMALS

What other animals can you see?

It depends where you live –
there aren't many elephants in England,
or polar bears in Mexico.

Made in the USA
Coppell, TX
31 March 2023

15023070R00076